ROAD MACHINES™

Snowplows

Joanne Randolph

The Rosen Publishing Group's
PowerKids Press™
New York

1

For Joseph Hobson, with love

Published in 2002 by The Rosen Publishing Group, Inc.
29 East 21st Street, New York, NY 10010

First Edition

Book Design: Michael Donnellan

Photo Credits: p. 5 © Corbis; pp. 7, 11, 17 © Highway Images/Bette S. Garber; p. 9, 13, 21 © Index Stock; p. 15 © Image Bank/Steve Niedorf; p. 19 © Image Bank/Andre Gallant.

Randolph, Joanne.
Snowplows / Joanne Randolph.
    p. cm. — (Road machines)
Includes bibliographical references and index.
ISBN 0-8239-6038-2 (library binding)
1. Snow plows—Juvenile literature. [1. Snow plows.] I. Title.
TD868 .R36 2002
625.7'63—dc21

                                                         2001000058

Manufactured in the United States of America

2

Contents

This is a snowplow.

4

5

Snowplows are big trucks.

7

A snowplow clears snow off the road.

9

A snowplow has a big metal blade in front. The blade pushes the snow to the side of the road.

11

Snowplows have special tires. Big treads keep tires from slipping on icy roads.

13

A person drives the snowplow. She is resting after a busy morning. She cleared a lot of snow. If it snows again, she will be ready to go!

15

Snow and ice make it hard to drive. Snowplows keep the roads safe.

Snowplows are
very important.

If it is snowing, snowplows will be at work.

Words to Know

blade

snowplow

treads

Here is a book to read about snowplows:

Snowplows
(Machines at Work)
Hal Rogers
Child's World

To learn more about snowplows, check out this Web site:

www.snowplownews.com/gallery.html

Index

Word Count: 102
Note to Librarians, Teachers, and Parents

PowerKids Readers are specially designed to help emergent and beginning readers build their skills in reading for information. Simple vocabulary and concepts are paired with photographs of real kids in real-life situations or stunning, detailed images from the world around them. Readers will respond to written language by linking meaning with their own everyday experiences and observations. Sentences are short and simple, employing a basic vocabulary of sight words, as well as new words that describe objects or processes that take place in the world. Large type, clean design, and photographs corresponding directly to the text all help children to decipher meaning. Features such as a contents page, picture glossary, and index help children get the most out of PowerKids Readers. They also introduce children to the basic elements of a book, which they will encounter in their future reading experiences. Lists of related books and Web sites encourage kids to explore other sources and to continue the process of learning.